WARFIELD PRESS

PRESCOTT, ARIZONA

TEA PARTY
OFFICIAL
HANDBOOK

A TACTICAL PLAYBOOK FOR
TEA PARTY PATRIOTS

America is worth it!

CHARLY GULLETT

"*Government is not reason; it is not eloquent; it is force. Like fire, it is a dangerous servant and a fearful master.*"

--George Washington

TEA PARTY TABLE OF CONTENTS

"One hand does not wash itself..."

Forward

"The problem is a lot of our people don't vote…" It was not meant to be a pejorative comment, just a simple statement of fact. I was having a phone conversation with my friend Bob Corbin. Bob has been one of the most outspoken presidents of the National Rifle Association in a long history of controversial Second Amendment advocates.

I had just finished doing a local radio show discussing the Tea Party phenomenon. Bob had heard me say how important it was going to be to get people active. We discussed at some length the idea of using the tactics in my book (_Cooking Alinsky's Goose_[1]) to train local NRA clubs how to be effective activists in turning around the trend toward Socialism in America. My comment was, "…Bob, we have to get out of the mindset that we can do it by ourselves." One of the principal success stories of the political left has been leveraging the Karl Marx concept of organizational coalitions into the American Socialist agenda, but Alinsky said it best…

> "…a wide-based membership can only be built on many issues…In a multiple-issue organization, each person is saying to the other, "I can't get what I want alone and neither can you…"—Alinsky[2]

The loose English translation on the facing page of the 1970's La Raza Unida poster is … "_One hand does not wash itself._"

Karl Marx, Saul Alinsky and La Raza Unida all understood this vital political concept. Obama rode into the White House in 2008 by using ACORN and other voter registration organizations to activate, register (and then delivered to the voting booths) such diverse constituencies as illegal immigrants, drug addicts, environmental wing nuts, pro-abortion groups, wealthy liberal elites, global warming alarmists, academic terrorists, animal rights activists, uninformed independents, unhappy Republicans, and anarcho-pacifist-anti-war flute hippies to name a few.

In response to this and all the Socialist intellectual and financial atrocities that have been implemented by the Federal Government since Obama took office, clear-thinking Americans (what remains of us) have taken to the streets in one of the largest grass roots protest movements in the history of Liberty and Capitalism.

It's called a Tea Party and it's a beautiful thing to see. Families, soldiers, farmers, musicians, small business owners, factory workers, ranchers, plumbers, everyday folks who have been inspired to stand up against the onslaught of political terrorism.

Obama, his White House criminals, and other Socialist operatives have called us crazies, racists, mean-spirited, Nazis, and mindless-cable-driven radicals. They say we have nothing better to do than to create an evil atmosphere of violent right-wing extremism intent in a Christian-Conservative-Republican profit-motivated program of preying upon the poor, helpless, victimized unfortunates in society.

This kind of leftist hate-speech is revealing.

If you actually listen to Tea Party participants, it is pretty clear we are all angered by what is going on and motivated to do something. The big question is what? Right now (Fall 2009) we are a large, unorganized group of patriotically-inspired, but politically unrepresented individuals. Although we are often disappointed by failure of the Republican party to stand up for our values, and routinely incensed by the intellectual bankruptcy of the Socialism that has taken over the Democratic Party, we lack a clear direction of where to go and what to do next.

The Tea Party organizers throughout America should get the Medal of Freedom for all the hard work they have done in getting us together, allowing us to realize we are not alone, and that we have a common voice when it comes to certain core values, namely...

- *Defending the Constitution of the United States of America*
- *Faith in Free Market Capitalism*
- *Limited Government protects individual Liberty*
- *Advocate Fiscal Responsibility in all things*

My local Tea Party organization (www.prescottteaparty.com) documented a mission statement to reflect those core values, realizing the values themselves are in conflict with actions by elected Socialist politicians who spend our money like there is no tomorrow and inject their transfer-of-wealth agenda into public and private activities for which there is no constitutional authority.

Prescott AZ Tea Party Mission Statement

Our mission is to organize, educate, and inform our fellow citizens to secure public policy consistent with our core values. We will unify and we will exercise through all legal means available to us, our power to effect the election of local, state, and federal candidates who espouse our core values.

This is great stuff...but how do we actually *accomplish* this? What specific steps can be taken that will truly effect public policy consistent with our core values?

Is it enough to get together, wave signs, sing patriotic songs, give rousing speeches and then, what...go home? Hope for the best? Buy a generator and put some canned goods in the garage for when it gets worse? How much worse does it have to get than to realize we are having these thoughts? Commiserating with like-minded patriots puts us in a nice comfort zone; but without a plan of action, without specific goals and metrics for success, without a tactical playbook, we are leaving the results up to the very people who put us in this position in the first place. Being nice and quiet, and being patient and assuming our elected officials and our political parties will do this for us is exactly how we got into this mess.

We can't afford to wait any longer. Now is the time for action, specifically for real down-home, old-time political activism directed at re-establishing freedom in America.

And that is why I wrote this handbook.

This is about what to do next, and _how to do it_. Specifically, this is a playbook for Americans who want to defeat Socialism and contribute to re-establishing the traditional freedoms of Liberty and Capitalism in America.

Although some of what is in this handbook is taken from what I consider to be the best of the activist material from my earlier book _Cooking Alinsky's Goose, The New Capitalist Handbook_[1], it is not a rehash of the "_Goose_". There is new material on starting Tea Parties, keeping them going and most important, what to do after the party is over and you have a thousand motivated patriots who want to go out and do something to save America.

Adding to my previous work on Voter Registration I have not only identified the specific issues of non-registered and non-voting voters but have now added new material on how to respond to those complaints and get them into the voting booth on election day.

I have broadened the concept of using Alinsky's tactical activism to include new information taken from other historical radical sources. Many of them are successful methods used by the Socialists to defeat American Liberty, and now we are going to use those success stories to _leverage Tea Party core values into public policy_.

As I have said many times, if we really care about Liberty, we need to take some pointers from the people that have been beating us like a rented mule with tactics that have successfully leveraged their Socialist agenda into American public policy. It is time to defeat Socialism once and for all.

This book will help you do that.

Part I: Tactics 101

> *"We should not reject the strategies of the political left just because they have been used against us by the enemies of Liberty. If we care about America and the inseparable relationship of Liberty and Capitalism, we need to embrace ANY realistic strategy or ethical tactic capable of success."*
>
> *--Cooking Alinsky's Goose* [1]

The first rule of activism is...there are no rules. The left is not playing by the rules, so we're not going to have any either. That does not mean the tactics presented in this handbook are to be construed as advocacy for illegal action or violence; they are not. The tactics of non-violent activism presents special problems for Socialists which they are able to more easily overcome if we use violence or other illegal activities.

In particular, non-violent activism creates empathy on the part of those middle-ground voters who are not yet on our side, often brings the despot's own people to our way of thinking, and makes it very difficult for criminal politicians to respond in any way that does not make them look like coercive tyrants.

Violence on our part also makes us look bad which adds fuel to the Socialist fire and can dissuade potential middle of the road recruits from joining our cause.

Having said that, let me point out the more daring the defiance, the more difficult it will be for the bad guys to ignore us without demonstrating weakness and fear of exposure; and in so doing they risk the possibility of more widespread defiance. This forces their hand, puts them into the classic trap of Alinsky's conflict/response model and puts us in the catbird seat. Violence gives them an out which justifies their own use of violence, which decidedly we do not want.

So be careful, there is a balance between the audacious and the illegal and each of us must stand on that line and decide what is personally ethical. There is dangerous information in this handbook that can get you jail time. In Minneapolis, I once heard Stephen Gaskin say, "...morals are defined by what you do when no one is looking." Inevitably the decision to do the right thing will be made by you and you alone.

Morality is on the side of American Liberty and we want to keep it right there. One of the problems is that in fighting Socialism we are up against those who are neither moral nor ethical.

> *...we face an enemy who believes one of his chief*
> *weapons is that none but he will employ terror..."*
> > --Wild Bill Donovan

Where do we go from here?

Instead of wringing our hands and hoping Socialism won't be too bad or that it will probably happen to somebody else, we are going to do some thinking "outside the box". I am going to suggest that as the Tea Party movement grows, there are tactical forms of non-violent activism which the left has used effectively against us and which we can now turn against them.

The FIRST TACTIC of ACTIVISM: As evangelists for Liberty we must LEARN to separate the political terrorists from the tactics of successful activism.

My theme, here and elsewhere, is this...changing the tide of Socialism in America is not about embracing the evils of the liberal left; it is about *recognizing their methods* and then finding ways to transform those methods into the defeat of Socialism.

When we see one little Socialist piss-ant sitting at home with a personal computer and helping to drive Gov. Sarah Palin out of office by generating 25% of all the ethics violations filed against her and costing the governor and Alaskan taxpayers millions of dollars to defend those charges, we need to quit waving our hands in the air and think, "Much as I hate it...that was a pretty good tactic. *How can I make this same tactic work for Liberty?*"

The SECOND TACTIC of ACTIVISM: We must identify motivated leaders.

There are qualities of organizers which are more useful than others, and while no handbook has room to teach those qualities, identifying who have them is critical to who will be more likely to succeed in turning Tea Party core values into public policy. No organizer ever has a full grasp of all these virtues, but the good ones have a *working familiarity* with most if not all of them.

As you read these over, consider this: these are the criteria the left used to recruit leaders to defeat us and are these not the qualities of seriously successful people everywhere? Indeed, are they not the qualities conservative business managers, retailers, small construction companies, bankers and corporate industrialists are constantly looking for in high achiever employees? Here they are in a nutshell...

Activist Virtues (after Alinsky[2])

- *Irreverence*
- *Curiosity*
- *Imagination*
- *Sense of humor*
- *Vision*
- *Organizational (task management) personality*
- *Knowing the difference between strategy, tactics and negotiated results*
- *Perseverance*
- *Flexibility*
- *A serendipitous sense of adventure*
- *A sense of the meaning of life*

No wonder liberals had trouble finding activists in their ranks with these qualities. Ironically, their search for successful activist leaders is actually based upon finding people with the very qualities which provided corporate America, successful farming operations and management in industry with a dependable foundation for financial success, and provided America with the backbone for Liberty and Capitalism. Even the notion of irreverence, while not taken literally by corporate managers, is often sought out as a virtue for perspective leaders. They just don't call it irreverence...they call it 'thinking outside the box.'

Thankfully, the issues of imagination, experience and the other virtues in organizing and managing organizations are far more familiar to conservative Americans with jobs than to Socialist welfare addicts. This was a problem for them; it's a blessing for us.

Business owners, entrepreneurs, hard-working blue-collar employees, designers, engineers, skilled workers and executives form the innovative and financial backbone of the American free-market economy. There would be little in any training program taught by Socialist activists that would appear new to us; in fact, most of us would think they had plagiarized our own training programs.

However this is not about managing small businesses or corporations, or knowing how to frame houses, or how to professionally sweat a plumbing joint or run a cash register (although all that is good stuff to know). Successful activism occurs on two very distinct and different levels; organizational and individual. Let me give you some good examples, starting with the next tactic.

The THIRD TACTIC of ACTIVISM: Successful political action is based on our ability to leverage political power through coalitions of diverse groups.

Political power in this case is defined as affecting real change in public policy. Here is an example of diverse group dynamics; the NRA throws a wide net for scarce funds during both good and bad economic times in order to fight legal battles at the state and national level that will impact our firearms freedoms at all levels. And yet, sport fishing (not specifically what the Second Amendment is about) is also an integral part of our economy and it is also an important wildlife management tool, both of which are important to the goals of the NRA.

During the 1930's when things were economically much worse than they are now, a coalition of sportsmen (which included the NRA, but embraced many other non-firearm organizations) banded together and implemented one of the most far-reaching public policy programs in American history. It was called the Pittman-

Robertson Act and it was put in place specifically for the benefit of all wildlife and habitat, not just shooters. Although the NRA benefited from this, they could not have done it by themselves; it required a grass-roots coalition of diverse groups who envisioned a goal larger and more important than their individual agendas.

Since 1937, hunting and fishing licenses have contributed an astonishing *4 billion dollars* through Pittman-Robertson to purchase millions of acres of public lands for the protection of wildlife habitat and to fund other important conservation programs. This is a success story of **coalition by diversity**, and we need to model this type of coalition.

So, if today the NRA wants to create a coalition of like-minded activists the membership list would need to include not only the NRA and other obvious Second Amendment advocacy groups like the Second Amendment Foundation, Jews for the Preservation of Firearms Ownership, and other likely conservative hunting groups like Ducks Unlimited, Safari Club International, National Wild Turkey Federation, Rocky Mountain Elk Foundation and Quail Unlimited, but diverse organizations like the American Legion, Special Forces Association, US Army Ranger Association, Fraternal Order of Police, etc.

If you could create a coalition of these groups and each of them _committed to providing a nickel out of every dollar in their budgets_ to defeat Socialism, you would have the financial foundation to work wonders. Remember, there is great power in the realization that if defeating Socialism isn't worth a nickel today, it won't be worth a plugged nickel tomorrow.

We need this coalition and others like it. There is much more on coalitions in Part II.

But, don't think it's all about big organizations. The other side of the coin is the individual activist. Hence…

***The FOURTH TACTIC of ACTIVISM: The strength of Liberty has
always flowed from the individual.***

During the late summer of 2009, I witnessed with absolute
amazement the effect two people had on the political process.
James O'Keefe and Hanna Giles walked into a few ACORN
(Association of Community Organizers for Reform Now) offices
with a hidden video camera posing as a pimp and an underage
prostitute. In the video, employees of ACORN are seen helping
them find low-income housing to run a prostitution ring, and
providing information on how to illegally get more underage
children into the country.

Every conservative person I know, every conservative pundit, and
even a few Republicans (those who had a spine left) had been
complaining about ACORN. Beck and O'Reilly brought down some
heat on their financial structure, but no one had been able to do
anything about them. Within weeks of the video release on FOX
News, both the US House of Representatives and the Senate had
voted to cut off billions of stimulus dollars to this corrupt
organization.

Two people accomplished this.

A final thought on the tactics of activism; there are people who say
we can't play the same radical game fomented by the Socialists and
if we do our ethics have been compromised in the process and we
have lost by definition. Today these people are legion.

NEWS FLASH...as of November 2008 we lost America to Socialism
and we lost it because they have been hitting us below the belt for
over a half century. There is no compromise in combat and *this is
absolutely real combat with the future of the free world at stake.* As
in the defense of our homes, our families and our lives, those who
would promote quiet, passive resistance are either innocents who
have never been in a real fight, are in denial regarding the realities
of Socialism, or are part of the conspiracy to destroy you.

There is nothing about hitting them below the belt in conflict with our core values. In fact, it can be said in the defense of Liberty, when a free people is engaged in a final struggle for truth, justice and the American way, hitting below the belt is a moral imperative. In the end, there is only one set of ethics, one virtue that is worth a damn and that is what you do to defend America from Socialism.

My sense is you cannot passively negotiate with the unwavering intent of evil. You **_can_** defeat it and here's how...

Part II: Organizing Coalitions

"...they had to stick together to keep us under control. And to maximize their strength they had to keep us divided. I learned early that when divided, the many become few."

--<u>The Making of a Chicano Militant</u>,
Jose Angel Gutiérrez[4]

From Marx to Alinsky to Obama, the Socialists have networked diverse groups into focused organizations in order to leverage political power. Our task is no different, their challenges are our own; what separates them from us is our core values.

Several things must happen in order for America to defeat Socialism...

- *First we must create and organize both local and national coalitions of rational diversity*
- *Second, we must use the coalitions to motivate and train their members in how to facilitate massive new voter registration;*
- *Third, we must leverage both House and Senate majorities in the 2010 mid-term elections by getting our people to the polls;*

- *Fourth, we must have a new Contract with America as part of the 2010 Republican platform designed to overturn the legislative tax slavery of the Obama program for Socialism.*

So, lets get going. The first item of business must be to create *local coalitions of rational diversity*, and then we need to organize national coalitions of the coalitions to create a purpose driven impact on everything from local and national elections, to healthcare, industry and education. The national coalitions occur at the corporate level, but just as important is the grassroots level, yep...your own back yard. Here is how to do it.

Backyard Coalitions

Every idea starts with one person, coalitions are made by getting someone else on board with you. Then you both work to get two more committed, then eight, etc.

The FIFTH TACTIC of ACTIVISM: Don't re-invent the wheel. Leverage existing communication channels in both personal life and business to provide a broad foundation for exchanging vital information.

This must be expanded as much and as quickly as possible. You already know like-minded folks whom you have seen, talked to and emailed. You already attend Tea Parties, and you belong to Republican political groups, church groups, shooting ranges, veterans organizations, parent/teacher associations, hobbyist clubs, sporting organizations and health clubs to name a few. Look at your email lists and the membership cards in your wallet; Hell, look at your Christmas list.

Create an Email distribution list.

Hopefully you will need a lot of computer space to do this. Don't want to clutter up your current Email? Need a FREE Email account with unlimited computer memory to do this? Point your browser to: https://edit.yahoo.com/registration and sign up. The new Yahoo not only provides you with Email, but also has live "Chat" features and texting capability for contacting people on their internet-enabled mobile phones (iPhone, Blackberry, etc.).

> *"Change comes from power, and power comes from organization. In order to act, people must get together...Power and organization are one..."*
>
> —*Saul Alinsky*[2]

Start a TEA PARTY

Tea Parties are happening with great regularity these days; invite a friend to join you, and then invite them to discuss the Tea Party and what you can do together. Add them to your Email distribution list and then find another person to join you. Be sure everyone is registered to vote (more on this later).

The SIXTH TACTIC of ACTIVISM: If you haven't got a Tea Party organization in your area, start one. Here's how...

- **Organize a meeting**. *Yeah, I know, everybody hates meetings, but it won't happen without them.*
- **Pick a location**: *start small with a few friends in your living room, expand as necessary. There are a wide variety of free venues in which to meet (not the least of which is the local watering hole), but the public library often has meeting space, VFW's, shooting ranges, sporting clubs, etc.*
- **Pick a topic that everyone can relate to at the meeting**: *you may have an egregious politician in town that needs*

ousting, or a particularly nasty little piece of legislation in need of defeat (like Obama's Mama-care), maybe your school board is out of control on some issue, and there is always voter registration.

- **Meetings are like Listerine...don't hold too many of them**. *In the case of planning direct public actions, three meetings are plenty; hold the first meeting to plan the event, the second to be sure everything is in place, and the third after the event to analyze how it went, how it could have been better, and how to use the new recruits you got from the event to effectively plan the next event.*

- **Organize activism**: *pick leaders out of your group to create and maintain a website, get someone started on a newsletter. Put someone you really trust in charge of finances. Appoint someone to be the media contact and then get everybody on the program that the media contact is the ONLY person who will speak to the media. Inevitably some things need to be printed (flyers, posters, etc.); find someone with experience that can do this, preferably someone already in the business.*

- **Hold a Tea Party Event**, *kickass, take names, get Email addresses, and sell T-shirts with pithy sayings. Hey...sell this book! Call me, we'll do sushi.*

Corporate Coalitions

This is the other level of coalition organization. We need corporate representatives to step up to the plate here. Here I use the word corporate in its widest possible sense (e.g., not only businesses but government agencies, church congregations, national 501/C3 charities, etc.). As with the individual, it must start with one person who finds another, then another...

The SEVENTH TACTIC of ACTIVISM: Leverage contacts in other corporations and agencies with whom you are already affiliated, currently do business and have an existing relationship with in order to get your foot in the door.

We need to find, communicate with and organize our fellow high achievers at the national level. I know many places have rules against doing this sort of thing; find a way around it. Start with your co-workers, and then go for your immediate supervisor. If you can get the president or CEO on board, so much the better; get them to provide letters of introduction to the corporate players in your industry who can be recruited to the cause. Use your business trips wisely; use your expense account with vigor.

An Historical Example

Here is an example of coalition activism we can use as a model. One of the left's creations in the late 1960's was the national Environmental Law Society (ELS), originally organized in the capitol of La-La Land, Stanford University, Berkley California. Still languishing today out of Boalt Hall School of Law at the University of California, Berkley, the ELS was initially created to network law students nationwide and originally included Harvard, Yale, Columbia, and George Washington University among others.

Their goal was to establish a network for volunteer environmental legal research assistance, sponsor environmental law conferences (in those days on Global Cooling in preparation for the coming Ice Age), and to publish and Environmental Law Review. They recognized this could not be done alone. They sought assistance from all the law schools involved asking for coursework to sensitize students to the issues, make faculty expertise available to targeted actions, institute interdisciplinary studies and to provide an outlet for testing their legal education by confronting legal challenges on a working level. They also publish a newsletter called (what else?) the *Treehugger*. The puppet-master now pulling the ELS strings is the Center for Law, Energy & the Environment (CLEE) at UC Berkley.

Eventually, in response to an accusation that Stanford itself was wrecking the local environment at Coyote Hills, they organized a coalition of diverse groups to defend their host including Sierra Club, Palo Alto Civic League, Committee for Green Foothills, Los Alton Hills Association, United Stanford Employee Housing Committee, and the Stanford Conservation Group. Note, these were not all environmental groups, but they were all stakeholders in the issue.

At that time, the groups also envisioned creating a larger national coalition of environmental action groups (what they thought of as an environmental A.C.L.U.). Instead, they simply injected climate extremists into Richard Nixon's newly formed Environmental Protection Agency and then stacked the EPA with radicals who then advocated their wing nut ideology as public policy.

It strikes me this makes a nice coalition model not only for current law students but for other conservative college students, to expose the fraud of global warming and other environmental issues and to counter any of the virulent Socialist agendas now pervasive in our schools.

Other entirely different but equally important coalitions must be organized. Here are some suggestions:

- *Paper-based publishing companies, libraries and News Organizations*
- *Website Alliances among small business, artists, designers, computer manufacturers, and ISP internet providers*
- *Ecumenical Coalitions with Bible publishers church-based construction companies*

- *Construction corporations with the Tool/Die Industry, Concrete, Wood suppliers and Architects*
- *Restaurants with the Cafeteria Industry, food and beverage Suppliers, along with commercial grocery chains, hotel chains and the Tourism Industry*
- *Any OEM with their suppliers and their end users*

What other coalitions can you think of? Once you have an idea for a coalition, what can you do to insure its success? Here again, we look to standard management tools which have been used by most of us to start, manage and perpetuate businesses.

- **Use your imagination:** *I mentioned earlier I think it is a powerful idea that if we don't spend a nickel today, it won't be worth a plugged nickel tomorrow. We must get corporations and conservative 501C3 agencies and small business to commit fractional but important funds to the cause. Get creative. "If freedom is not worth a penny today, it isn't going to be worth two cents tomorrow"...etc. Start by asking for a 5% commitment, if they can't do it, go for the 1% solution, but get some cash. Now is the time to sell something really important.*
- **Get your coalition partners to commit to providing contact lists.** *Using their employee lists and their corporate and agency contacts as channels for communicating information and getting further donations is a power tool in activism.*
- **Recruit your corporate trainers.** *These are really powerful individuals and can used to great advantage both locally and globally. We need training programs to both motivate and activate corporate employees to political action.*
- **Train the Trainers.** *This is a very powerful corporate tool to maximize training in any organization. One trainer trains a second, they train ten more, etc.*

- **Recruit artists and designers in the marketing department.** *We will need posters, sharp looking recruiting materials of all kinds, flyers, commitment forms, name tags, tons of things; turn these guys loose, you'll be glad you did.*
- **Organize your people and your coalitions into active Phone Banks, Email and letter-writing campaigns:** *this is one of the most profound mechanisms in politics, particularly just before elections. All corporations have enormous lists of customer phone numbers. Get them, use them. Motivate everyone to call, write and Email editors, politicians and businesses.*
- **Leverage your local and state legislature:** *these elected officials are typically more approachable (and more responsive) than federal hacks. Organize and get initiatives onto th ballots. Often initiatives at the state level can leverage public hearings and floor debates. If they are not responsive, target them for direct action.*

Think BIG. At some point, you will need to network with other corporate coalitions that are not in your industry but are on the same program for defeating Socialism. There is already a movement afoot to get everybody on board. Michelle Malkin, American Solutions for Winning the Future, Smart Girl Politics, American Liberty Alliance and others are partnering with http://teapartypatriots.org/ to organize and support a nation-wide coalition.

Join them.

Part III: Voter Registration

Want to do something important for American Liberty today?

The EIGTH TACTIC of ACTIVSM: Get your hands on a bunch of Voter Registration forms, put a packet of voting information together, and don't go anywhere without them.

Get over your shyness about asking people if they are registered to vote. We need a majority of people, and more importantly, we need a majority of *electoral states* to win elections.

If you read the "GOOSE" closely, you know there are approximately 25,000,000 conservative voters in America who were either not registered in the 2008 elections or were registered and did not vote. When you consider only about *8,000,000 votes decided* the Presidential election, voter registration should begin to fire your imagination. It is clear there are more than enough conservative voters out there to have reversed the election in 2008 if we could only have registered them and then made their presence known at the polls. We need to change this. Here's how...

Whether you are doing corporate training as part of a large coalition or out there on your own, there are some basic voter tools you need to use in order to deliver votes on Election Day.

- **Voter Registration Forms***: usually available from county voter registration offices (or similar government agencies),* *you should always have some in your car or truck, don't forget to keep some at the office.*

- **Proposition Packet**: *It's not just about candidates, there are usually propositions, grassroots initiatives, taxes, etc. that are on the ballot with the candidates. Here in Arizona, the elections board mails out an explanation of all propositions and candidate descriptions prior to the primary and the main elections. Get one, don't lose it. Be sure you are familiar with the issues and know what side you want to be on (this won't be hard) and be prepared to advocate that position. It makes you credible and people will trust you because you know this stuff.*

- **Voter Contact Forms**: *See the appendix for the format of this form and then use them to keep track of who you are registering, their Email, phone number, address, etc. Then use the data to re-contact them in an on-going process to keep them engaged with the issues.*

- **Poll Maps**: *Be sure to have an address list of the polling places and a map showing what areas are included in the polling areas and pinpointing the voting locations.*

You are going to meet a wide variety of people doing voter registration. The Tea Party event is crucial for both recruitment and voter registration as these folks will typically be fired up and motivated to do something at the end of the event.

The NINTH TACTIC for ACTIVISM: Be prepared to advocate voting to the non-voter.

As an Evangelist for Liberty you must be able to speak not only about the candidates and the various propositions on the ballet, but in particular you must be able to respond to the big question...why vote at all?

It is not unusual in many situations to meet people who are not voting. There are two nuts to crack in this situation; the 10% of registered Republicans who succumbed and voted for Obama's silver-tongued Socialism, and the registered voters who did not go to the polls. Both of these groups present different challenges, but they both tend to identify with similar rationalizations which motivate their actions. Here are some good comebacks to common complaints.

- *"I thought vice-presidential candidate was great, but I would die before I voted for an idiot like the presidential candidate."* You don't get one without the other and the enemies of freedom want your vote nullified. He may be an idiot, but he's our idiot and he is on the side of freedom. The alternative is to let the Socialist implement the largest government controlled transfer of private wealth in history. Things are already bad now, if you don't vote it is going to be far worse, not only for you but for your children, your grandchildren and their children.
- *"The candidate didn't show any spine in the campaign and in doing so he really let the opposition off the hook."* Try to show them that it is not about the candidates so much as it is about freedom versus tax-slavery. The issues are always larger and more important than the personalities involved.
- *"Another day another candidate; it's boring."* It may be boring in the light they see it in. It is a lot more interesting when you consider the stimulus, the deficit and Obama's Mama-care health control is going to bankrupt the country and everyone will suffer, profoundly, even those who are bored.
- *"It doesn't make any difference...they're all crooks. Screw 'em."* The biggest thief is the one who steals your right to vote. The crooks are in charge because good people chose to sit at home and not vote. You want to

really screw 'em, vote the SOB's out of office. No vote in our lifetime is more important than this one.

- **"The Republican Party is no different from the Democratic Party. Why vote?".** They are different; the Democrats have been taken over by the Socialists who have an agenda of controlling our choice in everything, from work to play, from our choices about immigration to our choices in health care, even our choice about what food to eat and what car to drive. The Democrat's stimulus money is the theft of your savings. There are big differences here, be prepared to speak to them.
- **"The Electoral College really elects presidents, my vote doesn't matter".** Every vote matters, even the ones who create Electoral representatives. Explain how 24 million votes who stayed home let 8 million votes put Obama in office.
- **"I'm retired, it doesn't really affect me anymore."** Oh yes it does, once the Socialists have bankrupted both the American economy and Social Security there will be no retirement checks and you won't be able to move in with your kids because they don't have a job.

The TENTH TACTIC of ACTIVISM: Be prepared to speak to the issues of UNREGISTERED VOTERS.

When you are confronted by someone who has clearly not registered in the past and therefore is clearly not going to be voting in the next election, realize _this is our biggest opportunity_. Here are some responses to their most common objections that will help you to get them registered and into the polls.

- **'My friends think voting is stupid'** – This is typically peer pressure acquiescence from young voters. Appeal to their adult qualities in making a decision on their own; America has always rewarded those who in time of crisis were able to rise above the noise of the foolish crowds and make the tough decisions for the right reasons. Voting is the mature expression of a free person.

- **'The candidates are not interesting'**–"It's not about caring for the person, it's about being interested in the issues that deeply affect your life today and the opportunities they are stealing from your future and your children's future."
- **'I don't know where to register'** – Get out your Voter Registration Packet, help them find their polling place, show them where it is on the map and offer to help them find it before the election. Offer to mail in the registration for them and then fill out your Voter Contact Form.
- **'I'm kind of intimidated by the whole thing'**– Try to create some rapport, offer your own experience in going to the polls. "I will help you. "
- **'I can't read or write very well'** – Tell them you don't have to write anything except their name. Tell them that the law allows them to have help in the voting booth. Offer to help yourself or offer to find someone they trust who will help them.
- **'I am self-employed and I can't take the time away from work'** – Explain the "Vote by mail" absentee voter process.
- **'I don't want to do jury duty** – Explain to them they are already on the jury duty list as it is also drawn from DMV drivers license lists.
- **'The Voter's Guide is overwhelming; I don't understand the propositions'** – Get out your *Voter Guide* and be prepared ahead of time to explain it in plain English.
- **'My boss will kill me if I leave work'** – Explain their workplace is required by law to allow them the time to vote. As an alternative to a boss who threatens such things, there is also absentee voting or vote on the way to

or from work (polling places are typically open 7 a.m. to 8 p.m.).

- *'After all the talk about 'hanging chads' I'm afraid to make the wrong choice'* – Again explain you can have someone help in the voting booth, or they can ask for a new ballot if they make a mistake. They can also choose to vote at home and take their time with someone to help them fill out the ballot correctly.
- *'I'm not getting involved. All the negative campaign ads make me want to puke'* – This is exactly what the Socialists want them to do...stay home. Explain that low voter turnout is exactly what got us into this mess and the more people who accept it, the more negative it is going to become.

The ELEVENTH TACTIC of ACTIVISM: Interim re-contact is critically important with new voters.

Political rallies such as the annual Patriots Day events, Tea Parties, or community service events sponsored by Rotary, VFW, and women's groups can all be useful opportunities for re-contact with new voters. This type of thing will bring folks back from the edge. Organize a voter fun day at the local shooting range, golf course or racket ball court. Identify community and commercial meeting places and then organize a pot luck dinner or bake sale. If you can afford it, rent a bus. At a minimum, be sure to call these folks back the week before the election, remind them who you are, arrange to pick them up if necessary and then **_deliver these voters to the polls on election day_**! We must leverage our activities and our networks into poll participation. We cannot do this without you. Every rational American must make a commitment to locate, register and then deliver to the polls this lost sea of conservative voters. Use your imagination; use your feet.

Part IV: Direct Action

"The leftists may still have a chance—by default...
Historically, we are now in a kind of intellectual no
man's-land—and the future will be determined by
those who venture out..."

The New Left: The Anti-Industrial Revolution
--Ayn Rand [5]

I am tired of watching Socialist criminals trash everything American patriots have worked and died for in the last two centuries. We have all had one or more members of our family pay the ultimate price for our Liberty. The theft of this Liberty is an insult to that sacrifice.

It bears repeating; it is the greatest crime of which an elected politician may be guilty; to coercively legislate a confiscation of wealth in order to perpetuate the poverty of entitlement and the nationwide establishment of Socialism. This theft of American wealth is fueled by tax money directly and indirectly through inflation, taking it from those who worked for it, and giving it to those who don't.

This is Socialism.

I've said it before...Socialism is treason. It is criminally motivated political terrorism. Both terrorism and treason are anathema to Liberty and those who advocate it are political criminals. This is not complicated. Clear-thinking Americans must begin to view Socialism as a prosecutable crime and recognize those who conspire to advance it are in fact criminals to be adjudicated in courts of Federal law. We must embrace the notion our Founding Fathers defined high crimes because they are real, they are being perpetrated against America and they need to be prosecuted. We cannot let them take over through 'default' because we did not at least stand up and try to turn this around.

This irrational assault on Liberty must end and it has come to our generation to take care of business.

What I am about to suggest is highly controversial, I wouldn't want you to think it is anything else. I would submit that what the Socialists have already done and are about to do, not only to us but to future generations of Americans, is even more controversial. While we must leave prosecution to lawyers, we need not wait to make the lives of Socialists and their mindless minions as miserable as possible.

Let's look at some of the situational tactics they have used and see if we can't use some of these strategies to our advantage. By way of example, let's begin with the issue of the environment. The strategies and tactics I suggest for them can be a model used by you for other targeted groups. First a little background on the green weenies.

The History of Green Radicalism

> "...the conservation movement, though it operates within the law, is in principle revolutionary."
>
> <u>ECOTACTICS</u>--Paul Brooks [6]

When I was a young buck in the 1960's, ecology was often the topic of the day, second only to the Viet Nam war. But in those days the pseudo-science was not setting their hair on fire about global warming, in those days the alarm was about global cooling; the coming of the next ice age (these guys will never get it straight). The United States eventually succumbed to the whacky persistence of irrational beatnik lemmings and in the 1970's passed new legislation such as the Clean Water Act, the Clean Air Act, the Endangered Species Act, and the National Environmental Policy Act; all are foundations for current environmental standards.

Although small, hard core (deep-ecology) extremists with single-agenda activism like *Earth First!* struggled for recognition (and then went to jail), the diversity of the movement was and continues to be their greatest challenge. With private citizens, professionals, fringe religious wing-nuts, irrational politicians, questionable pay-to-play "scientists" and violent extremists in the mix, it is not surprising their agenda is somewhat fractured.

Greenpeace activist Steven Guilbeault put it this way, "...global warming can mean colder, it can mean drier, it can mean wetter." [8] I am so glad Greenpeace finally settled that whole warming thing for us. Does the word *lunatic* leap to mind here? Enough of this, I feel like I'm kicking a dead planet or something. Let's look at the tactics they used to create this nightmare and how we might inject a little serendipitus-interruptus into their agenda.

The TWELFTH TACTIC of ACTIVSIM: Successful actions necessarily require news coverage.

I think everybody knows by now the main-stream media is the mindless lap dog for the Socialist agenda. That they are in the tank for every liberal, ninny, and anti-American idea would seem to be in conflict with the goals of our Twelfth Tactic. However, one of the things I learned in journalism class is it doesn't much matter whether the news people are saying good things or bad things about you; what matters is *they are talking about you at all.*

This does not mean all bad press is good press, but it does mean that for the near term, bad press is likely to be the only press you will get for doing the right thing. At some point, if there are enough citizen actions against a particular organization, no matter how many biased, slanted articles they write, eventually even the terminally dim will begin to realize something is up and start asking questions. Let's look at a specific action used effectively by the tree-huggers.

San Francisco Bay Blues

One of the early environmental actions in San Francisco was focused on the bay area itself All the wing-nuts went down to the bay with cotton bank bags, filled them up mud and then delivered them to pre-determined corporate targets who they intended to vilify as culprits in polluting the bay. What made this action work wasn't the mud; it was the news media who covered the story.

They recognized the need to provide the media (in advance) what they believed were the facts which created the situation, the culprits to whom they were attaching guilt, and the demands they hoped would be achieved by the activism. Inherent in this media strategy was Saul Alinsky's most famous political tactic: "Pick the Target, freeze it, personalize, and polarize it."[2]

Was it coincidence reporters were standing on the steps of the corporate headquarters involved? Of course not, the activists had contacted the media before the event took place so that everybody was on the program. I have personally witnessed actions where the demonstrators actually contacted both the corporations involved and the appropriate police department so that sandwiches from the corporations would be ready for the demonstrators and the police had extra employees on hand to process the arrests.

Very cozy.

Big action or small, the media (and others) will be on the program for you (willingly or not), but you need to line up the media ahead of time. Newspaper coverage is good, radio is better; Network TV is worth more than all the zinc from Al Gore's Tennessee mine.

Additional methods of disseminating information include Tea Party events where you provide speeches, hold debates on public policy, and inform the public on what the targets are doing. Internet Blogs, pamphlets, house to house canvassing, petitions, Guerilla Theater and popular songs using new lyrics to satirize the target are all good communication methods to get your message out.

Knowing the Enemy

In order to target something you have to have some sense of what they are doing and when they are doing it. Inside information can be very useful and their employee newsletters frequently have schedules. Many employees throw newsletters into the trash and these can be retrieved from the same place.

Greenpeace is a good example: environmental whack-jobs have websites, often with Email Alerts and RSS feeds directly to your computer! How convenient and it is far less smelly than a trashed newsletter with yesterday's anchovy all over it.

The THIRTEENTH TACTIC of ACTIVISM: Sign up or subscribe to your target's internet alert service. Good research equates to good activism.

Well-planned actions have well-researched plans. Don't want to junk up your personal email, get a free one from Yahoo.com at https://edit.yahoo.com/registration. Use the resources I outlined in Appendix A...libraries, internet, etc. Research gives you the knowledge and the framework for the action. You supply the imagination. For instance, without too much effort you will discover the following information about Greenpeace.

Greenpeace owns an enormous ocean-going vessel which they use for various nefarious activities. Currently loose on the Pacific they are attempting to track down Environmental Pirates (better known as honest, hard-working commercial fishermen). Can you imagine the size of the carbon footprint this tub is pumping into the atmosphere and the ocean? This is like killing whales to save the seals.

The real agenda is anti-technology, anti-capitalism activism, the net result of which will put fisherman out of work and put their families in jeopardy. These idiots are so committed to the supremacy of the environment that they would let a fisherman's child starve so they can worship some fish they believe is telepathically communicating Rachel Carson's directions on saving the planet to endangered butterflies in Bangkok.

In February 2001, Greenpeace issued a press release blasting genetically improved "golden rice," the enhanced crop that could save hundreds of thousands of Third World children from blindness and death. Greenpeace has also been raising a stink about the growth of the biotech fisheries industry.

A handful of innovative businesses have learned how to genetically improve certain salmon species to make them grow faster, again contributing to the world's food basket, and Greenpeace will have none of it. The group is doing all it can to frighten consumers of this new product, and working behind the scenes to have it banned before it can even reach to marketplace.

The group has warned that genetic crop engineering would cause new and horrible food allergies (it hasn't), and that biotech corn would endanger monarch butterflies (whose numbers have increased substantially since the introduction of biotech corn). And completely forgotten by these dipstick "Frankenfood" protesters is again the tremendous potential for biotech foods to solve many of the Third World's famine-related problems.

Wonder of wonders, it turns out Greenpeace is heavily invested in the organic foods industry. When their green hysteria regarding bio-tech foods drove consumers away from those products in Brazil, the Greenpeace bottom line got fat by simultaneously promoting their organic food products.

The FORTEENTH TACTIC of ACTIVISM: Good planning is critical.

When planning an action a skillful choice for the point of attack is vitally important. In forensic debate, one concentrates on the most vulnerable part of the opponent's argument, not their strength. Similarly, do not try to hit an array of issues; pick one good one, isolate it from all others, put the face of an individual on it to personalize it, and then polarize the individual and the issue. Stay focused. Martin Luther King Jr. found in Albany GA in 1962 that not focusing on a specific issue resulted in failure to direct their energies effectively.

> *"...we decided that one of the principal mistakes we had made there was to scatter our efforts too widely...We concluded that in hard-core communities a more effective battle could be waged if it was concentrated against one aspect..."*
> <u>Why We Can't Wait</u>—M.L. King,
> (The New American Library, 1964)

Stay away from generalized arguments and issues such as peace, brotherhood, or freedom. You can mention these things but they cannot be the targeted issue itself. Arguments which are too ethereal or complex will not only be lost on your target but likely lost on your people as well.

> *"The issue must be definite and capable of being clearly understood and within the power of the opponent to yield."*
> <u>Non-Violent Resistance</u>—M. Gandhi
> (Dover Re-issue, 2001, ISBN: 0486416062)

Always have multiple exit plans prepared for each phase of an action including a bailout in the beginning if things clearly are not coming together. Having arranged your strategies, you now plan the specific action. It is necessary to determine in the beginning whether this is to be a planned public action with pre-press publicity (don't forget to get the permits), or a hit and run. In either event, it is imperative that you and/or your organization are not compromised before, during or after the action. Political and organizational survival is the key thing; you must live to fight another day even when you are faced with failure.

Several obvious field tactics are necessary (refer to the "Goose"[1] for additional information).

- *Your ability to leverage surprise and this can protect your people as well...*
- *legal but ruthless treachery disorients the opposition and disrupts their agenda...*
- *repeated action divides and overcomes their organizational and operational ability. The target should <u>not</u> be allowed to sleep thinking all is well. Hit them, hit them again, and then hit them again...*

- *Try to have a good time doing this; don't forget the real beer and brats after the event.*

Putting it all together...

So, how can we use all this information to our benefit? Irony and ridicule are great political weapons. With all the effort made to hide the ugly underbelly of these criminals, it is sweet to see them exposed.

- *A good activist slap in the face for Greenpeace would be to have people show up at a pre-arranged time (with dutiful notification to the media) and Scotch tape pictures of starving children on the Greenpeace building. Get pictures from the web, type "starving child photo" into any web-search engine.*
- *If you have a budget, next spring rent a dump truck, collect everybody's fireplace ashes and have a carbon party on the front lawn of the home of the president of Greenpeace. Stick a sign in it that says "Carbons 'R US" and tramp through it and leave nice carbon footprints everywhere.*
- *Get your computer printer to print some Avery labels with the same picture of starving children along with the Greenpeace logo and paste them on organic food products at the local hippie food outlet. Pick out the ones in which Greenpeace has invested.*
- *For their next fundraiser, print out small posters advertising a FREE MEAL at their benefit event, sponsored by Greenpeace and using their fundraiser location, date and exact time. Post them at welfare offices, drug rehab centers and low income neighborhoods and grocery stores.*
- *Greenpeace is a 501(c)(4) non-profit corporation, "Goose" them ala Alinsky with their own rulebook. Let's organize about, oh say 100,000 caring people to file anonymous IRS complaints (see http://www.sendanonymousemail.net/, be*

sure to copy Greenpeace at info@wdc.greenpeace.org), and do it on April 15th just to make the point clear. The complaint can say that they are not in compliance with IRS statues which prevent Greenpeace individuals with a financial stake in the corporation from having their private interest's furthered (called inurement in court). Any amount of inurement revokes their tax-exempt status. The bulk anonymous Email should really make the day special for our friends at IRS as well.

I'm sure you're beginning to get the drift on this, so let's look at another example of really good skunk-stink activism. How about our election nemesis, the politicians from the Democratic-Socialist Party?

Targeting Politicians

Again, use information from the "Goose" to both research and plan your action. Need information on topics important to your target? http://www.democrats.org/rss.php will feed it to your computer automatically. The main website has a swell feature called "Party Builder" which allows you to find groups, events and Democrats involved in your Zip Code. You gotta love these web designers; they want to be soooo helpful. In fact, they want to help so much that you can create your own Democratic Party event right on the site by simply filling out an online form.

Now let's see, what kind of event would we like to see them host? I like the idea of a FREE BEER event, how about you? In fact, let's kill two birds with one stone. Our local wing-nut here in Prescott Arizona is a long-time Democrat by the name of Ann Kirkpatrick who refused to attend our local Tea Party on Health Care. I'm sure Ann would like to host our little beer fest. Let's use her website: http://kirkpatrick.house.gov/ to find a good location. We see she has set up offices in Prescott, Casa Grande and Flagstaff, all swell places. Oh look, they have her schedule on here too!

- *As with Greenpeace, you can print out small posters advertising FREE BEER and pizza at all the Kirkpatrick offices statewide, sponsored by Ann and the Democratic Party of Arizona. Post them at welfare offices, drug rehab centers, low income neighborhoods and grocery stores.*
- *Have your people print up fake stimulus checks with the words "OVERDRAWN" in red. Paste these all over Kirkpatrick's offices statewide and hand them out at the event.*
- *Let's get a video camera and microphone and meet up at one of her photo-ops. We can ask some hard questions, like "...Rep. Kirkpatrick would you support criminal penalties including jail time for politicians who violate their oath of office or for those who act outside the powers delegated to them by the constitution?"*
- *Did you send President Obama a tea bag? How about we send about a ton of Kool-Aid packets to your local Socialist politician?*

Other successful traditional elements of non-violent activism may include:

- **Stand-Ins**: *This is where you get a large number of people to simply stand in the doorway and block entrance to an event you don't care for (Democratic Party fundraisers, etc.). Have a Bible in your hand and when they try to force you to leave tell them you are praying for them (and this is a First Amendment violation of freedom of religion)*
- **Sit-Ins**: *Frequently used in the 1960's, it gets your program on the news, can find you some new recruits but can also get you some quality time in jail.*
- **Form Overloads**: *Can you imagine the slowdown in the IRS taxation machine if in April we ALL filed a delayed tax*

return, then finally overpaid our taxes by $1, and then filed for overpayment refunds? Or how about we organize a nation-wide campaign to send in requests for membership information to the DNC (all the same week)?

- **Noise-Ins**: *Organize the use of noise-makers at a Socialist event; tiny bells, flatulent devices, horns, etc. and then get everybody to go to a speaker event. Every time they open their mouth, you light one off.*
- **Walk-outs**: *If there are any Republicans left in Congress with some spine, it would be nice to see them execute a mass exodus from the U.S. House and Senate floors on some "neutral" legislation. It strikes me a walk-out on Obama's Mama-care bill would also be in order.*
- **Economic Boycotts**: *Used effectively by La Raza and the United Farm Workers, we can do this as well. We need to leverage our coalitions to identify small business and large corporations, agencies and non-profit groups that are on our side and then we need to vote with our wallets and our support for these people. If a business won't support the effort they need to be targeted for economic boycott. Silent agitators can be very useful here.*

In this, and indeed all cases of good activism, it is important to compound their difficulty in extracting Socialist taxation, frustrate their efforts, limit their ability to gather funds, and continually expose these idiots for the deluded, intellectual frauds they have always been. The central foundation of these tactics is exposure through irony and ridicule; they fear these words, particularly ridicule.

> *"Ridicule is man's most potent weapon. It is almost impossible to counterattack ridicule...it infuriates the opposition, who then react to your advantage."*
> Rules for Radicals—Saul Alinsky[2]

The Kool-Aid packet is a case in point. Bill O'Reilly, our acerbic pal at Fox News, has turned a tragic event in American history (the Jim Jones congregation mass-suicide with poison-laced Kool-Aid) into what is now a well-recognized and humorous bit of ridicule; the "Kool-Aid drinkers". As a result of Bill's efforts, virtually all references to drinking Kool-Aid are now associated with fraud and self-delusion which are the hallmarks of Socialist argument. By "connecting the dots" we necessarily associate the former with the latter.

The FIFTHTEENTH TACTIC of ACTIVISM: Be prepared. (Okay, I swiped this from the Boy Scouts, but it's a good one). The media can be a little thick between the ears and you must be prepared to connect the dots for them.

This shouldn't be too hard, after all you thought the action up in the first place, but keep it in mind when you talk to the media. Make these connections for them. In particular when you are trying to attract a news reporter to come to the event and cover your action, it will help sell the events newsworthiness to his editor. So explain the carbon ashes connection to carbon footprints and liberal fraud that supports them. Be prepared to speak to the issue of anti-technology movements that result in starving children here and in the third-world countries. And when you bury a politician's office or photo-op event in Kool-Aid packets your media person should be prepared to discuss the psychosis of Socialism.

Don't get trapped into regurgitating a lot of statistics. Statistics are good metrics in the classroom, students take notes and they can be tested on what they remember. When talking to the media IT IS BORING. Most normal people (those math-challenged patriots who are not business majors) go brain-dead when they hear statistics. This is not to say they are bad people, but like Pavlov's dog, they have been bludgeoned by a legion of poor math teachers and counselors who told them this stuff was for accounting students.

THIS IS IMPORTANT...It's not about statistics, or math or even the dollars involved...to motivate people they must actually see the threat in terms they understand...you must tell them about the loss of hopes and dreams in their life. These images must be real to them.

Instead of saying the Cap and Trade legislation is going to "...cost your family between $1500 and $4500 a year," you need to tell them <u>what it is they are going to lose</u> by not having that money in their life, e.g. the vacation they hoped for this year is going away, the second car they hoped to have as a graduation present for their high school senior will no longer be a reality, and for people already in economic trouble, they are not just going to have margarine instead of butter...they are going to first get dry bread and then no bread at all in order to make sure the baby gets milk.

Part V: Final Thoughts

"Collectivism (aka Socialism) has lost the two
crucial weapons that raised it to world power and
made all of its victories possible...reason and
morality...the collectivist dropped them because
they had no right to carry them. Pick them up...
You do."

<u>The New Left: The Anti-Industrial Revolution</u>
--Ayn Rand [5]

Socialist ethics are enamored of irrational, coercive and psychotic philosophies which when implemented through public policy and Socialist governments have historically resulted in massive poverty, wide-spread suffering, loss of individual rights, loss of private property, altruistic tax slavery and death-squads.

Every liberal propeller-head from Rev. Jeremiah Wright to Minister Louis Farrakhan, from Woodrow Wilson to Barack Hussein Obama has fallen prey to these intellectually bankrupt ethics and in doing so have become the committed enemies of all rational people who believe in individual freedom. They do this because as individuals they are *afraid and alone* in their political madness even when surrounded by large numbers of their own kind.

Many of their leaders were raised in their formative years without loving care-givers, poor care-givers or care-givers who abandoned them and this creates in them a pathological perception of life's solutions as dependence on big government (see _The Liberal Mind, The Psychological Causes of Political Madness_ by Dr. Lyle H. Rossiter, Jr. M.D. ISBN: 978-0-9779563-0-2). According to Dr. Rossiter, this dependency leaves liberals...

> "... with residual infantile longings for a return to effortless gratification in the care of an omnipotent benefactor...latent longings of the masses to re-experience the guaranteed security of an idealized parents care...The liberal politician exploits whatever developmental deficiencies remain from those years by promising to allay our most basic fears; we need only give him enough power and money to do so".

In a nutshell, that is the basis for all totalitarian ideology. Socialism preys upon fear to garner votes for implementation of a violence-controlled, fear-based, nanny-state; it legislates from a position of fear in order to confiscate wealth through taxation and violence; and it uses _fear of violence_ to control those who will not bend to their will.

Right now, many of us are also afraid, but for different reasons. We are afraid of what has happened to America in the last century of growing dependence on government intrusion on our private lives, the leviathan growth of social-welfare, the non-stop attacks on the U.S. Constitution and our enumerated liberties in the Bill of Rights, incipient implementation of terror by the enemies of freedom inside America. We are afraid of what the Obama administration is planning and implementing that will create tax slaves out of our children and grand-children. We are afraid of the Socialist strategy to condemn us, to vilify us and to marginalize patriotism. We must overcome this fear.

One of the most famous non-violent activists in history was a little guy name Mohandas K. Gandhi (often referred to as the Mahatma or teacher). Gandhi frequently spoke of the importance of transforming this condition of fear and willingness to submit, into fearlessness and self-respect as an important requirement in liberating people from tyranny.

Similarly, another well-known American non-violent activist, Martin Luther King Jr. once said during a bus boycott in what was then a repressive Montgomery, Alabama, "...a once fear-ridden people have been transformed. Those who had previously trembled before the law were now proud..." The historic and powerful results of both Gandhi and King are well documented; in both cases profound social and political changes were brought about.

In fact, Socialism, like other repressive governments, is dependent upon sources of power which are largely vulnerable to non-violent activism, e.g. material resources (both financial and political), human resources at the local and regional level, mass submissiveness on the part of officials, submissiveness on the part of the people at large, instruments of legislation dependent on rulebooks, the pomp and circumstance of public office, the need to leverage expensive social programs through large slow-moving bureaucracies, party allegiance and absolute control of information. These are their weaknesses and are now our strengths.

There are always three stages to any totalitarian takeover, specifically *Manipulation, Possession and Confiscation.*

Manipulation occurs over a prolonged period of time where the instruments of public communication and knowledge become propaganda vehicles for political fraud (e.g. school curriculums, print/electronic media), political party platforms are conspicuously compromised, and voter blocks are created out of the ignorant, the disenfranchised, the wealthy liberal elite, academic lapdogs, and the criminal outcasts of society.

Possession arises when they are able to leverage groups like ACORN into transforming these voter blocks into election victories. Election victories give them the illusion of the parental security they never had, and the illusion sustains the aphrodisiac of power.

Finally, in holding the reins of power, **Confiscation** of both public and private wealth transpires. First this happens through inflation (which directly robs your personal wealth by decreasing the value of your savings and investments), and then by the furtherance of power through outright taxation (cap and trade, health care you don't need and don't want, stimulus packages that don't stimulate anything, shovel-ready jobs that don't have any shovels, etc.), as well as other forms of confiscatory legislation which eventually result in enormous state-supported bureaucracies, national bankruptcy and tax slavery not only for ourselves but for untold generations of our children.

As I write these words, Socialists are already firmly ensconced in the second stage of political Possession.

Historically, when a nation allows itself to reach the third stage, non-violent activism turns into public violence, the democratic-legislative process turns into a fraud of puppet theater, law enforcement turns into violent repression, people pick up guns or pitchforks or whatever is left as a weapon and _both the guilty and the innocent pay the final price_. This process is a well-worn Socialist formula which has been used throughout history and always ends the same way.

Fortunately we are not yet in the third stage and there is time to turn things around. But...we are out of time to simply hope things will change, to assume if we wait long enough someone else will figure out a solution. We are definitely out of time thinking political criminals like the *Twelve Monkeys of Socialism* (i.e. Barrack Hussein Obama, Nancy Pelosi, Harry Reid, Barney Frank, Chuck Schumer, Barbara Boxer, Sheila Jackson Lee, Hillary Clinton, Diane Feinstein, John Conyers, Harry Waxman and Joe Biden) are working in our best interests; they are not.

Two centuries ago rugged individualism, inspired by the notion of owning and controlling our own destiny, stirred to action in a beautiful but dangerous wilderness, Americans forged out of their imagination the only moral government in history. Backed by a Constitution and a Bill of Rights, founded on the notion that rational governments serve the people and not the other way around, colonial patriots wrought with their intellect, their bare hands and their blood, the most profound political change in the history of the world.

The task of defending Liberty has passed from parent to child through every American generation since 1776. Today it is in our hands.

Do with it what you will, but whatever happens, I invite you to stand with us. If you haven't been to a Tea Party, please go...you will find yourself in good company

Appendix A: Resources from the "Goose" [1]

I have already discussed how the left drove Gov. Palin out of office by using numerous false ethics charges to sap time, money and energy by using the Alaskan Ethics Book against her. There is no reason why we can't make the same strategy work against the enemies of Liberty. Pick any Socialist idiot you want (Republican or Democrat).

The list of US House of Representatives members is available at: http://www.house.gov/ and can be accessed by typing in your Zip Code. Check this out. The House has their own ethics committee and all kinds of rulebooks that can accessed and then used against them at the following website:
http://ethics.house.gov/Pubs/Default.aspx

These manuals are currently available from the House Ethics website...

2008 House Ethics Manual
Highlights of the House Ethics Rules (PDF Document)
Code of Official Conduct
Committee Rules

US Senate members are listed by state of residence at:
http://www.senate.gov/

Here is the website for the Senate Ethics Manual...
http://ethics.senate.gov/downloads/pdffiles/manual.pdf

Here are the current members of the Senate Ethics Committee
(111th Congress)...

DEMOCRATS:	REPUBLICANS:
Barbara Boxer (Calif.), **Chairman** and Ranking Member	Johnny Isakson (Ga.)
Mark Pryor (Ark.)	Pat Roberts (Kan.)
Sherrod Brown (Ohio)	Jim Risch (Idaho)

There are well-honed tools of activism from which we can draw
both experience and data. Whether you intend to operate alone or
within the context of a coalition of friends or organizations, you
will find time is against you. When I was at Intel Corporation, a
common saying was "...work smarter, not harder". Let's look at
some of the tools available to save you some time.

Public Records Research

Thorough research cannot be overstated. The government leaves
paper trails like slugs leave goo. Public records can be a gold mine
of information both in terms of alerts to government action as well
as evidentiary material to legal proceedings, but mining that data
can be arduous and gaining access to it can be challenging. In 1974
the Freedom of Information Act (FOIA) was passed by Congress
with the understanding that the law "...is based upon the
presumption that the government and the information of
government belong to the people." Alinsky's fourth rule of power
tactics was to make the enemy live up to their own book of rules.
The FOIA is one such rule book. Currently the Department of
Justice maintains a website with a compilation of contacts for
everyone in the government who handles FOIA requests and is

categorized by agency. This site is currently located at:
http://www.usdoj.gov/oip/foiacontacts.htm.

It is important to understand that there is no central office in the government which processes FOIA requests for all federal agencies. Each agency responds to requests for its own records. Therefore, before sending a request, you should determine whether the agency you are contacting is likely to have the records you are seeking. Other general sources of information about how to make a FOIA request include: "Your Right to Federal Records," available for fifty cents per copy from the Consumer Information Center, Department 319E, Pueblo, CO 81009. This publication also can be accessed electronically at:
http://www.pueblo.gsa.gov/cic_text/fed_prog/foia/foia.htm

"A Citizen's Guide on Using the Freedom of Information Act and the Privacy Act of 1974 to Request Government Records." This report is published by the Committee on Government Reform and Oversight of the House of Representatives. It is available for sale for $5.00 from the U.S. Government Printing Office, stock number 052-071-01230-3. It also can be accessed on the World Wide Web at:
http://www.tncrimlaw.com/foia_indx.html

At the federal level of government are all sorts of information holdings that can be useful. The Federal Communications Commission (FCC) requires and catalogs information from companies and individuals involved in licensed television, radio, and cable TV stations. For instance, the FCC can provide information on La Network Campesina, a radio station which is part of a larger network of stations supporting illegal immigration (http://www.campesina.com), and is one of the most rampant border anarchist broadcasters here in Arizona. La Network Campesina is a huge network which grew out of the Corky Gonzales farm workers movement.

Other federal resources for research include the Federal Reserve Board (located on the web at http://www.federalreserve.gov) , National Labor Relations Board (http://www.nlrb.gov), and the Federal Energy Regulatory Commission (http://www.ferc.gov). Contributions to federal elections are recorded and available from the Federal Elections Commission (http://www.fec.gov).

Presidential candidates must also file contribution information in the states where they spend money. Candidates typically have campaign committees which must also divest themselves of information through public record, usually available from your Secretary of State Office. Congressional directories reveal who is lobbying in Washington, again available through Worldcat.org at your library or purchase online. Personal finances of US Senators are filed with the Secretary of the Senate, Office of Public Records (SOPR at http://www.senate.gov). Lobbyists also register with the Senate Office of Public Records in accordance with the Lobbying Disclosure Act (LDA). Lobbying and other records are available for public inspection.

Grass Roots Research

You will find a great deal of information regarding a wide range of subjects at your local county recorder's office. The recorder's office does just what it sounds like; records documents, as required by law, which are part of the public record. Documents recorded include real estate transactions, mortgages, deeds of trust, family trusts, personal property, tax liens, mining locations, subdivision plats, records of survey, military discharges, official appointments of office, and other documents required to be made of public record. Many of these documents will be available in paper form, or in the case of earlier historic records may be available in microfilm. Here in Arizona, by legislative statute the Recorder's Office is also in charge of Voter Registration (get those voter registration forms from these guys).

Our county government also has an extensive Global Information System (GIS) with digital mapping of our entire county including overlays of property and not only who owns the property but who owned back into recorded history (I'm not kidding). These systems can be correlated to embarrassing back-tax information and sale of property for non-payment of taxes. The GIS is available to the public via an internet website which also offers the entire county agency service network. Both street and rural mapping information is incredibly useful when planning activism.

Other local agencies are also capable of providing you with useful data. The Socialists have been beating us over the head with "...pick the target, freeze it, _personalize it_, and polarize it". In many cases you will be looking for personal information on individuals. The local coroner's office may be able to provide data on relatives of deceased citizens; spousal and maternal maiden names are two of the most common aliases. Salary, job title, tenure, retirement benefits and sometimes work history of government employees are listed with various civil service agencies, personnel departments or state comptroller's office. You can really create havoc with an individual by simply knowing where they work and calling their personnel office pretending to be an employer who has received their application for a job; that little zinger will go back to their boss about thirty seconds after you hang up (don't forget to use a public phone). This is called social engineering.

Don't forget the newspaper. Local, county and state law enforcement agencies routinely place arrest information in the newspapers (the big arrests make it on local radio). New corporations are required to place public announcements in the newspaper; business licenses while not necessarily incorporated also appear in the paper. The obits are full of data.

When it comes to individuals, you will eventually bump up against privacy laws, many of which were enacted at about the same time as the FOIA. A useful library text on this subject is the *Compilation of State and Federal Privacy Laws* available in many public libraries. If you want one for your own reference it is available on Amazon.com (where else?). The current version was published in 2002 and contains a 2009 Supplement (ISBN: 9780930072179).

Libraries

If you don't have a library card, you are missing the whole point on information. A very valuable reference in the library is called *Business Information Sources.* Now published by the University of California Press and in its third edition (October 12, 1993) you may also order this reference online and in good used condition can sell for only a couple of bucks (ISBN: 978-0520081802). It not only contains information on how to use libraries as research vehicles for information but includes important information on time-saving resources and specific information on finding information on corporations, organizations, businesses and individuals, and industrial research.

Libraries also typically keep a copy of *Standard and Poor's Register of Corporations, Directors and Executive*, as well as *Dunn and Bradstreet Directories.* Libraries also have enormous inter-library resources. Your local and state court system will also have public records on arrests, convictions, divorce, law suits, criminal records, and probate.

Appendix B: VOTER CONTACT FORM

☐ Name:

☐ Email Address:

☐ Phone Number:

☐ Hot Button Issue:

FOLLOWUP: Get confirmation on these items...

☐ Voter Registration Completed and MAILED

☐ Confirm Email

☐ Confirm Phone

☐ Hot Button Issue

Interim Re-contact:

Date

Date

BE SURE THEY KNOW WHERE THEIR POLLING PLACE IS LOCATED

☐ Polling location for this voter:

☐ Confirmed transportation on election day

warfieldpress.com

References:

[1] *Cooking Alinsky's Goose, The New Capitalist Cookbook*, Charly Gullett, Copyright © 2009, ISBN: 978-0-9841559-0-3, by Warfield Press, Prescott Arizona

[2] *Rules for Radicals, A Pragmatic Primer for Realistic Radicals*, Saul David Alinsky, Copyright © 1971, Softbound ISBN: 0-394-71738-8, by Vintage Books Edition, March 1972

[3] *How to Beat the Democrats And Other Subversive Ideas*, David Horowitz, Copyright © 2002, Hardbound ISBN: 1-890626-41-4, by Spence Publishing Co., Dallas, Texas

[4] *The Making of a Chicano Militant*, Jose Angel Gutiérrez, Copyright © 1998, Softbound ISBN: 0-299-15984-1, The University of Wisconsin Press, Madison Wisconsin

[5] *The New Left: The Anti-Industrial Revolution*, Ayn Rand, Copyright © 1970 by Ayn Rand, The New American Library, Inc., New York, NY

[6] *Ecotactics: The Sierra Club Handbook for Environmental Activists*, Copyright © 1970 by The Sierra Club, Softbound ISBN: 6761-77233-3, by Signet Pocket Books

[7] *Green Rage: Radical Environmentalism and the Unmaking of Civilization*, Christopher Manes, Copyright © 1990, Boston: Little, Brown and Co.

[8] *Let's keep our cool over global warming*, Ed Feulner, TribLIVE website, Copyright © 2005 TribLIVE News, Pittsburg, PA

About the Author...

Charly Gullett was originally trained as a photo-journalist in the U.S. Army Defense Information School. However, he spent most of his adult life as a self-taught applications engineer specializing in Robotics, Digital Instrumentation and Analog Computer Design. Retiring in 1996 from Intel Corp. as a senior technical author, Gullett was awarded their highest individual achievement award for his ground-breaking work in Artificial Intelligence. Additionally, his career has included work as a professional photographer, cabinet maker, college teacher, a firearms dealer, and a professional artist who has illustrated over thirty books. He has also authored one previous book on political activism as well as two books on action shooting and gunsmithing.

WARFIELD PRESS

PRESCOTT, ARIZONA